I sat down for my breakfast

Richard Andrews

Not just a Dad, a loving father

Happy Birthday

CONTENTS

Illustrated by Charlotte Brown

The Slug

I sat down for my breakfast; a couple of pieces of toast,
There is, I think, no better food in which to get engrossed.
But as I drank my cuppa I peered inside my mug;
Goodness me,
What should I see?
A big fat juicy slug.

"What are you doing there?" I asked. "And how could it come to be
That come this Friday morning, I find you swimming in my tea?"
I addressed the slug quite calmly in case it should be scared,
But none of that
As up it sat
And solemnly declared:

"I used to live in Lincolnshire where farmers grow great crops
And one day accidentally, I was transported to the shops."
But as he spoke his words were slurred and he seemed more and more
confused,
The side of his head
Was slightly red
And rather badly bruised.

So I gently asked "Are you all right?" with obvious concern,
For there were no other symptoms that I was able to discern.
With tender care I picked him up and felt his swollen glands
And with a frown
I put him down
Because he left slime upon my hands.

The Slug said "Oh, you're very kind; you make my life much easier,
But I fear I've received a blow on the head that's given me amnesia.
It must have been in Sainsbury's something knocked me to the floor,
It was maybe a cabbage
That did the damage
And I can't remember any more."

The sadness in the Slug's big eyes made him appear to be quite old,
But despite my heartfelt sympathy, my toast was getting cold.
So I took a few big mouthfuls in something of a hurry
Then said: "Have no fear,
I've a great idea,
You've no more need to worry."

I pointed out the window saying "See that yonder hedge?
Just next to that is my kitchen garden where I grow a load of veg".
So I took the slug and set him down by the radishes and the leeks
And he ran amok
Amongst my stock
For weeks and weeks and weeks.

Then one day sometime later whilst I was tending my spring greens,
I found my slimy friend and said: "Brother Slug, how have you been?"
He replied: "I love your vegetables but now very few remain
And now I yearn
For a quick return
To Lincolnshire again."

"You don't want to go back there," I said, "and live upon a farm,
You know all those funny things they spray can do you terrible harm."
He said: "Yes, the farmer's chemicals are something quite appalling,
But every night
When I turn out the light
I can hear my homeland calling."

Reluctantly I told the Slug I'd accede to his migration
And that if he packed his luggage I'd take him to the station.
"There'll be no need for that," he said. "Though thank you all the same,"
Because behind a leaf,
To my disbelief,
He'd built an aeroplane.

With a marrow for the fuselage and wings of runner beans
And with wheels made out of Brussels sprouts; it was an extraordinary machine.
"Can it really fly?" I asked and the Slug said: "Let this suffice…
What's really cool
Is the bio-fuel
That powers the device."

"And might you have?" The Slug enquired as he found a leaf to stand on,
"Somewhere where the ground is firm for me to take-off and land on?"
"I know just the place," I said, "down by the potting-shed."
Then he said something unclear
That I couldn't quite hear
As he put his goggles on his head.

Then he sat inside the cockpit and started up the jets,
Flames leaping from the trembling machine, singeing my courgettes.
He taxied to the potting-shed; the whole garden seemed enthralled.
What a sight,
This pioneer of flight;
A mollusc to inspire us all.

The Slug shouted: "Wish me luck!" above the engine's sound,
And as the machine raced past the watering can, the nose lifted from the ground.
The noise became a deafening roar, exhaust fumes everywhere.
My best artichoke
Was enveloped in smoke
As he swept into the air.

The engine's noise grew fainter as the cloud slowly cleared
But when once more I could see the sky, the Slug had disappeared.
Perhaps he made a new home, maybe underneath a hedge?
Or was his fate sealed
In a lonely field
In a mass of tangled veg?

Then last Tuesday by my front door, sitting on the rug
I found a slimy letter sent from my friend, The Slug.
"I've been around the world a dozen times," he wrote disarmingly
"But of all the places I've been
And all the things that I've seen
Home's the place for me."

The Zoo, Daddy

Sitting at home, rather bored, with nothing much
to do,
When with a surge of inspiration I cried: "Dad,
let's all go to the zoo."
"The zoo. The zoo." He said, "There's not much
there to see,
I'd much rather stay at home and have a cup of
tea".

"But there are lions" I cried, "and tigers too and so many other creatures,
Just think of all those animals with all those funny features".
"Come on," he said. "Get your coat; I've got a good idea.
If it's animals you're after, I know some very near."

So we walked a while hand in hand then Daddy suddenly stopped and said:
"There's one of those animals we've come to see: it's a zebra, crossing
ahead.
See the stripes of black and white; they're quite a considerable size.
See the way all the cars slow down when they see its orange eyes."

"Oh, Daddy." I said. "I know about that and that's a rotten trick you've
played.
You made me think we'd see animals…" and with that, I stormed away.
"Hold on, come back," my Daddy yelled. "Don't get in such a stew,
Let's go home and get Mummy, then we'll all go to the zoo.

THE FLY

Buzzing round and round the room
There's a large and noisy fly,
I have an urge to squash it
There is no reason why.
As it lands upon the window
I pick up a copy of *Hello!*
A hearty swing and a heavy crash,
And I've flattened the little fellow.

A shock, a horror,
beyond any words can say;
The fly that I had previously
squashed
Is back again today.
"Hello!" I said. "Is it not you
Whose head I smeared against the glass
And now you're back again today,
How can it be this comes to pass?"
The fly replied: "Twas I indeed and by your hand
My little head went splat,
But try again you ugly brute
Cos you'll have to do better than that."

I could see this fly was very tough
And that I hadn't hit it hard enough
So I paused for a moment to reflect
On the outstanding strength of this insect.
With its infernal buzzing in my head
I set about, as you'd expect,
To catch the thing and send it packing
Straight from this world to the next.

"Ooer!" said the fly quite clearly,
"There's something I must mention:

I see that bashing me upon the head
Is unmistakeably your intention".
"Of course it is," I shouted back,
"It's because you are a pest;
You lay your eggs in nasty places,
Spread diseases and the rest".

Thereupon, without ado
I duly set about
To chase the fly and trap it
And deliver a fatal clout.
With my largest hammer in my hand
It mattered not a jot,
That I was smashing up the house
As it flew from spot to spot.
Another swing, another crash,
A hole in the kitchen door,
And with another mistimed swipe,
My wife's unconscious on the floor.

But then at last I had it
Between the sideboard and the Hoover
I'd trapped it in a little space
With no room to manoeuvre.
First the abdomen, then the thorax,
Then finally the head,
This time there would be no mistake;
I'd make certain that it's dead.

"Hey, Mister! Not so fast."
The hairy creature cried.
"There's something that I'd like to say,
Before you commit insecticide."
"OK, little buddy, carry on,"
Half expecting a cunning trick.
"But I ain't in no mood for jokes,
So nothing fancy and make it quick."

Then the fly stood up quite proudly
And straightened up his tie.

"All right," I said. "What is it?"
And this was his reply:
"I'm not here to be a nuisance
But food's the thing I need,
You see, back at home I've got a wife
And hungry maggots to feed.
I've been watching you quite closely
I see you've children of your own
What would life be like for them
If suddenly *they* were left alone?"

I stroked my chin and then I said:
"Well I respect your point of view,
We need to formulate a plan
And this is what we'll do…
If you'll agree to leave me be
And not come buzzing round my ear
I'll let you go, even though
I'd rather squash you here,"

And just as we agreed the deal
My wife started coming round
(You may remember that she'd been left
Unconscious on the ground)."
Are you all right, my dear?"
I asked my darling wife,
But other things were on her mind
As she grabbed the carving knife.

With a movement that I barely saw
The blade went flashing from her hand
And it took me not a second
To see where it would land.

"No!" I screamed "Not the fly."
But the aim was straight and true,
As the knife hit the wall with a gentle thud,
It sliced the fly in two.

Woe the poor fly that was cut in half,
Did you think it might survive?
How could it be that the little thing
Could not escape alive?
Well all that stuff about the knife
Was just a little joke
And the fly returned quite safely
To all his family folk.

(Perhaps all God's little creatures
Are in need of some protection
Even though they don't do much
To warrant our affection).
Now the fly, his wife and maggots
Have their lives to lead,
They live in someone's rubbish bin
Where they have all the food they need.

My Bouncy Yellow Ball

It came from cousin Oswald
From his travels in Nepal;
The greatest toy in all the world
My bouncy yellow ball.
Whenever Oswald came to stay
(Not often, as I recall),
We'd go to Barley Park and play
With my bouncy yellow ball.

It seemed to bounce so very high,
It gave me such a thrill
Up and up, it kissed the sky
As we climbed up Barley Hill.
"Cousin Oswald, watch!" I cried
As I clasped the yellow sphere
And running to the steepest side
Said: "Let's bounce it over here!"

I gave the ball an almighty throw
And it took off down the slope,
We laughed and laughed and watched it go
Like an Olympic champion antelope.
We took pursuit at such a pace
Dashing past old Barley Hall
Ever-laughing as we gave chase
To my bouncy yellow ball.

As we ran we couldn't help but see
All sorts of happy people, playing happily:
A Frisbee flew through the air
Caught by a boy with ginger hair,
A girl skipped gaily on the grass
Barely noticed as we dashed past,

Boys played cricket by a tree
With their mother as a referee,
Four young girls with hopscotch chalk
Hop and play and laugh and talk,
A shuttlecock is whisked away
By a breath of wind from the summer's day.

Yet still, the yellow ball we chased
Our footsteps didn't falter,
And how our endless laughter increased
As it dived into Barley Water.
And as we stood there by the pier
And let our laughs subside
My bouncy yellow ball appeared
Washed in upon the tide.

"I wonder if," I said to Oswald
"It's magic after all.
It's the greatest toy in all the world
My bouncy yellow ball."

MARY HAD A LITTLE LAMB

Mary had a little lamb
Whose wool was green and blue,
Mary didn't like the colours much
So she put it in a stew.

Mary had a little lamb
She put it in a stew;
It didn't cook for long enough
So it was very hard to chew.

Mary had a little lamb
She put it in a stew;
And when she'd finished all of that
She had some pudding too.

SAMMY, THE AEROPLANE BOY

When Sammy was but a little boy
There was nothing more that he'd enjoy
Than to stand and gaze up at the sky
Watching aeroplanes go by.
Perhaps it was their easy grace
That made a smile light up his face
And that they flew on without falling
Was something that he found enthralling.
He used to watch the thin, white lines
Stretching out from their behinds;
It made them look like they had tails
But really they were vapour trails.
Sammy didn't want guns that spat out flames,
He didn't care much for video games,
He didn't want Lego or electric trains;
He just wanted aeroplanes.

So on those days when it was cloudy
He'd stamp his feet and shout out loudly:
"Begone big clouds, you spoil my view
And I've got nothing else to do."
And with frustration rising to a great crescendo
He'd bang upon my bedroom window
And to his mother's great despair,
He'd run round the house in his underwear.
Thus it happened once that a layer of cloud
Hung over the earth like a ghostly shroud
And even though the weather forecast
Solemnly said that the cloud wouldn't last
The sunless greyness thus remained
So Sammy couldn't see any aeroplanes.
He shouted loudly: "It's just not fair!"
Then ran round the house in his underwear.

His Mother looked on, quite distraught.
His Father scratched his head in thought
And averting his gaze from the television,
Announced: "I've made a big decision."
He grabbed his hat and coat and scarf
And said he'd be home in an hour and a half.
Then to Sammy he said: "I'll give you a whack
If you're not wearing trousers when I come back."
He got into the car; a battered old Ford,
Turned the key and the engine roared
And as he reached the end of the drive,
Sammy looked at the clock: it was 4.45.
He went and stood beside the walnut tree
And craned his neck so he could see
His Father driving off into the gloom,
Then he trudged off slowly to his room.

He wondered vaguely where his Dad had gone,
And once he'd put his trousers on,
Sat down to read a magazine
Till Father's return at 6.15.
As said time came Sammy went to wait
For Father by the garden gate,
But with still no sign at 6.53
He went inside dejectedly.
Father was so much later that expected;
He hadn't even called or texted,
But then, at last, at 7.25
Sammy heard the car upon the drive
And as he peered around the curtain,
Saw Father push the front door open
And coming down the stairs he saw
Father place a bag onto the floor.

"I'm glad to see," Father started,
"You put on trousers once I'd departed
And I must also say to you,
I'm sorry that I'm overdue…
But I've been searching from store to store
To find what I've been looking for:
The thing to quell your deep frustration
That's caused by a lack of aviation.
But I think I've found the very thing."
And passed the shopping bag to him.
Sammy's eyes stretched big and wide
As he took the bag and peered inside,
But he couldn't see as well as he might
Because Mother was standing in front of the light.
Sammy revealed the package bit by bit
And there, in his hands, was an Airfix kit.

THE HOUSE ON THE BAY

The rising sun lights the eastern sky
And steals away the night,
It bathes the bay as it rises high
In the richness of its light.

The hours of the day tick slowly past
Lo! The climbing sun.
Higher and higher, the ball of fire
Beats on everyone.

The breeze provides a breath of cool,
The shadows a little more;
The sea sparkles like a diamond jewel
As it whispers to the shore.

The mountains in the distance
Reaching high and spreading wide,
There's no shade of green that can't be seen
Blanketing their sides.

The tide presses in towards the land
And yonder lonely beach:
It's left a ribbon of sun-bleached sand
Where its fingers cannot reach.

Clouds approach on the trade winds
Heralding the rain,
And with sudden power, a tropical shower,
Then the sky turns blue again.

The colours of the Isle of Spice
Make the brightest mixture;
The beauty of this paradise
Creates the perfect picture.

The sun dips over the horizon
And darkness begins to fall,
Thus ends the day on Westerhall Bay
And Lobster Lodge has seen it all.

MIRROR MIRROR

Mirror mirror on the wall
I've just had a nasty fall,
Mirror mirror you can't see
The little graze upon my knee;
Mirror mirror you're so small
You can't see that much at all;
Bang, crash, Big One Smash,
You are now out in the trash;
Mirror mirror in the bin
You can't see a single thing.

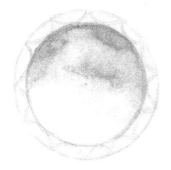

HOLDING HANDS

When I was a baby
Quite some years ago,
My Daddy used to carry me
Wherever we would go.

Now that I am bigger
And I walk mile after mile
I hold hands with my Mum and Dad
And that feeling makes me smile.

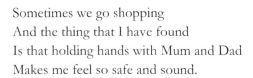

Sometimes we go shopping
And the thing that I have found
Is that holding hands with Mum and Dad
Makes me feel so safe and sound.

But when we get to busy roads
Where the traffic is quite frightening,
I'll be holding hands with Mum and Dad
And I can feel my fingers tightening.

When we're waiting at the crossing
For the car, the lorry and the bus
I'll be holding tight to Mum and Dad
Until they stop for us.

All those four-wheeled monsters
That pass so rapidly
See me holding hands with Mum and Dad
And they know they can't get me.

So one day when I'm older
I'll think back to when I was nine,
How when I reached for my parents' hands,
They reached out for mine.

THE WOODLOUSE AND THE CENTIPEDE

The garden is a peaceful spot,
It's quite my favourite place;
I can sit amongst the hollyhocks
With the sun upon my face.
But over near the garden shed
Where the sunlight cannot touch
Is a fearsome, terrible polyped
That no-one likes that much.

It lives its life beneath the stones
In a land as dark as night,
Where all its little neighbours' bones
Are quivering with fright.
It has no hair, completely bald
And moves at tremendous speed:
So what's this awful creature called?
The Common Centipede.

It has no eyes
But will paralyse
Its victims with one bite,
And gobble them up
Without a stop
To quench its appetite.

One day a woodlouse was traversing
Across the centipede's domain,
And he could hear the centipede cursing
Because he'd missed his lunch again.
Now the antennae of the centipede
Could feel the moving air
As the little woodlouse did proceed
Into the centipede's lair.
"A meal, a meal!" the centipede cried,

(the woodlouse none-the-wiser),
With venom ready to be applied
As a woodlouse immobiliser.
And as he drew in for the kill
He rose triumphantly,
But suddenly felt rather ill
And slipped and hurt his knee.

"Aargh, the pain,
Not that again.
I've done that twice before."
And the woodlouse stopped,
Rolled himself up,
And lay still upon the floor.

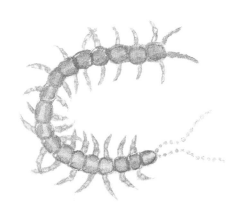

So the centipede who couldn't see
Or detect his prey's location,
Retired to treat the damaged knee
With a soothing embrocation.
So feeling fragile, like a chicken's egg,
He lay there, quite inert,
You see, he had more than one hundred legs
And he could not tell which hurt.

Now the woodlouse sensed the danger passed,
And carefully uncurled
And standing atop a fresh worm cast,
Stopped to survey the world.
But the woodlouse was a kindly sort,
Who'd once trained to be a nurse,
And he could see that the stricken centipede,
Had taken a turn for the worse.

The woodlouse yelled:
"The centipede's felled
And is looking quite pathetic;

Someway, somehow…"
The woodlouse vowed:
"…I'll administer anaesthetic."

Knowing the centipede could not see,
(remember centipedes are blind),
The woodlouse rather cunningly
Approached him from behind.
With a hypodermic ready
The woodlouse knew he'd got 'im,
He held the needle steady…steady…
Then he stuck it in the centipede's bottom.
The centipede's screams were unintelligible:
All bewilderment and surprise,
And but that it was not possible
He'd have had water in his eyes.

But he could feel a change a-coming
And a smile replaced the frown
Because the knee pain was a-numbing
And the swelling was going down.
And now the pain had all but passed
And with feelers probing every crack;
Was the woodlouse now within his grasp?
Yes, he'd make a tasty snack.

But to remain
In that place again
The woodlouse knew was crazy,
So he'd made his escape
In tremendous haste
And was now asleep…under a daisy.

I sat down for my breakfast

SOLDIERS

A tribute to the NHS

When the world was just a primordial mess,
The oceans fizzed and effervesced,
Volcanoes boiled with heat untold
And microbes began to get a hold.
Then despite the terrible air pollution
Began the process of evolution
And slowly, surely, life on earth
By degrees became more diverse.
It's something that we should be taught
(And to cut a very long story short)
Two billion years ago eukaryotic cells
Discovered that they could excel
And in a scientific way
Became the foundation of all life today.
Plankton, worms, bugs and snails,
Grasses, trees, birds and whales;
Of all the life that proliferates
Humankind now dominates.
Treading somewhat heavily
On all the things we humans see,
Without a pause to stop and wonder
The precious resources that we plunder,
And in our quest to go and get
We haven't built a safety net.

****

In the sea, on land and in the air,
Viruses are everywhere;
Thousands of species now persist
And happily we co-exist
But indeed there are a dangerous few
That knock us back with colds and 'flu.
Now December 31st Twenty Nineteen
Is a date we'll wish we'd never seen
For in Wuhan, China, great despair:
A new virus had been reported there.
And this new virus that appeared
Was of a character to be feared.
And then this tiniest, vile microbe
Began its spread across the globe.
The threat to humans quite immense
And foolish humans with scant defence.
On occasion but a mild infection
Not needing medical intervention,
Sometimes the patient was mildly sick
And with luck would recover pretty quick,
But others would be gravely ill
And for some, COVID 19 would kill.
Governments cry: "Stay apart,
For human contact gives the virus heart;
Stay at home, stop the spread
Forsooth there will be thousands dead."

****

World leaders tell us this is war
That we must fight with all our core,
They talk about the enemy
And how we must win victory.
But who are the soldiers in the fight?

Who will battle day and night?
Who will grit their teeth and snort
Derision to the foe's onslaught?
Who will selflessly embrace
The virus and its deadly face?
Who will fight on without rest
With courage pinned upon their breast?
Who will never, ever tire
In the face of unrelenting enemy fire?

Well, there's an army fighting now
With sweat upon their furrowed brow.
Fighting to hasten sweet reprieve
To patients who can barely breathe;
To calm the fever, soothe the cough,
To try to see this virus off;
To treat the helpless lying there,
To deliver unstopping intensive care.
So to the doctors and nurses so resolute
To you, it is, that I salute.
It's you who'll bring an end to slaughter
And lead us all to calmer water.
So how can we adequately express
Our thanks to you, the NHS?

I sat down for my breakfast

THANKS

This book is not being published for the purpose of profit, it is trying to make a dream become reality.

Proceeds made from the sale of this book will be donated to mental health charities in our local area, mental health has been at the forefront of our family for numerous years now and has impacted all of our lives massively.

Printed in Great Britain
by Amazon